DIAGNOSIS

Diagnosis is a contemplative and candid account of what one faces with the knowledge of a serious illness. These poems are delivered with the moving voice of a mother, wife, poet and professional charged with the will to make sense of the senseless. Lapidus reminds us of the brilliance and beauty in ordinary things, through senses now heightened by the impediments of ontological diagnostics, and the failings of the body: "The child-proof medicine bottle / so many shades of blue." Because of these dualities, or in spite of them, we are called upon to see the full beauty of life. These graceful poems celebrate the power of art and language and remind us that even in the darkest hours, "The fancy hotels of memory" will grace and enlighten us.

Cynthia Atkins
Author of *Psyche's Weathers* and I*n the Event of Full Disclosure*

ɞ

With the same generosity of spirit as Audre Lorde's landmark Cancer Journals, *Diagnosis* affirms the power of witness and of life itself. These poems bear the marks of a deep courage—the ability to speak the truth, to grieve, and finally to understand that "By looking fear in the eye / welcoming it / We learn that we are stronger than it seems." Whether joyfully recalling her daughter's birth or detailing the tough, day-to-day realities of cancer treatment, Lenora Lapidus gives testimony, clear-eyed and open-hearted, to "the healing power that pain can bring." I am profoundly moved by, and grateful for, the gift of these poems.

Elisabeth Frost
Author of *All of Us*

DIAGNOSIS

LENORA M. LAPIDUS

LEAKY BOOT PRESS

Diagnosis
by Lenora M. Lapidus

First published in 2013 by
Leaky Boot Press
http://www.leakyboot.com

ISBN: 978-1-909849-06-8

CONTENTS

Acknowledgements

I would like to thank all the friends and family members who were so supportive to me after my diagnosis in 2005 and who have continued to assist me over the past eight years as I confronted new obstacles, including my illness during the winter of 2012. In particular, I thank my loving husband Matt Bialer for standing by me through so many difficult times – when my father died shortly after we started going out 25 years ago, when I learned I had breast cancer, when my mother died in 2009, and last year when I was homebound for many months. I am grateful to be alive and am happy to have just celebrated our twentieth wedding anniversary. Matt truly lives up to the promise he made to me standing under the chuppah that beautiful August evening in the Berkshires: to love and support me through good times and bad, through sadness and happiness, in sickness and in health.

I thank my friends Karen Dublin, Carla Savetsky and Eve Kupferman with whom I've been friends for 40 years and who have supported me even as they had to confront their own health issues and life stresses; Rebecca Abrams who sat by my side, nursed me to health, made me a schedule for my medications, and took Izzy shopping at IKEA on Sundays so Matt could have a break and I could rest; Audrey Stone who first helped me understand how the cancer had spread through my bones and later brought me meals and took me to Kolot for spiritual support; Phil Tegeler who took walks with me and sat by the lake helping me perceive cancer as a chronic illness not a death sentence, shared a friendship deeper than I ever could have dreamed, and helped me become a better poet; Jenny Atkins and Bill Kinder who heard an early draft of these poems during one of our visits to Berkeley and with whom we have shared many fun, family vacations; Megan Galvin, Paula Bernstein

Orkin and Sarah Adelman who cheered me up with moms' nights at the movies and shared childrearing sagas as our daughters grew from young children into tweens starting middle school this year; Sharon Guskin who came to sit with me and talk books and music, and connected me to filmmakers, always seeing my strengths even in my weakest moments; Maria D'Albert who helped me explore my social entrepreneurial ideas and always admired my passion and energy; Laura Gilkey who came with me to Gilda's Club and helped me through those early days when our babies were young; Luisa Orto and Fraser Symmans who have been friends for decades and provided expert medical advice through each new phase of treatment; Beth Frost and Derek Hackett for their friendship and for Beth's talented edit of prior drafts of these poems and her offer to review this manuscript; and Kate Gyllenhaal who demonstrated her capacity for caregiving when Izzy fainted and who has promised to help me regain the physical strength and flexibility I had before my back bones were impaired.

I thank my relatives Maxine Rockoff who visited me almost daily last winter bringing me comfort food, telling me stories and sitting with me while I rested so I wouldn't have to be home alone; Lee Langbaum, Sam Beinhacker, and Teddi Hunter who have become not only my second family but my close friends; Irving Bialer and Thelma Bialer who have been like parents to me, providing love and support through everything; David Bialer, Mary McNear, their children, Roni Fontaine, and Michael Gill, who accepted me into their family as a sister and supported Matt through the hard times; Kyle Lapidus, Tali Hinkis, and their children, Jesse Wind, Connie Wind Walker, John Walker and their son, my extended family who provided medical information and support after I was diagnosed and again when I got sick, and who have loved me through many difficult times.

I thank Rabbi Ellen Lippmann, Cantor Lisa Segal, and the members of Kolot Chayeinu who provided me with spiritual support and nourishment when I was sick and in need of healthful food and loving kindness. I thank Lee Albert, Archa Hodges, Rosy Mann and all the other healers at Kripalu who have helped restore my body and nourish my soul through difficult times before and after my diagnosis. I thank Lorraine Massey who came to my house to cut my hair before I began chemo and has been with me every step of the way. And I thank Anthony Romero, Steve Shapiro, Louise Melling, Women's Rights Project staff, and all my colleagues at the ACLU who have enabled me to have such a fulfilling career and have given me the leave necessary to heal in times of need.

I thank Matt Volm, my incredibly talented, creative and kind oncologist who treated me from the time I was diagnosed in May 2005 through July 2013 when he left NYU Clinical Cancer Center. Dr. Volm cared for me during the ups and downs of remission and resurgence, modifying treatment protocols to fit my idiosyncratic responses to various drugs. Through it all, he treated me with respect, not simply as a patient but as a partner in my own healing. When he told me he was leaving NYU, I cried and thanked him for all he had done. He responded, "It was YOU! I would say JUMP, and you would ask HOW HIGH?"

I thank Jennifer O'Grady and Cynthia Atkins for their beautiful and inspiring poetry and for agreeing to read and review this manuscript; and Seb Doubinsky for his friendship and for recommending that I submit this manuscript to Jim Goddard.

Most of all, I thank Jim Goddard, Publisher of Leaky Boot Press, for offering to publish this manuscript and for understanding precisely what these poems mean to me. His keen eye and compassionate soul are evident throughout the production of this book.

******

I dedicate this book to my mother Leah Blumberg Lapidus and my father Ivan Richard Lapidus who provided me with the love and support to develop all aspects of myself and grow into the adult I have become and each of whom died far too young and thus are not here to share with me the celebration of this book's publication and of my current good health.

I also dedicate this book to my husband Matt Bialer who is the love of my life, my best friend, and my most trusted partner on this long and complicated journey of life.

Most of all, I dedicate this book to my beautiful daughter Izzy Lapidus who is the source of my strength to carry on.

Two Chinamen, behind them a third
Are carved in lapis lazuli,
Over them flies a long-legged bird,
A symbol of longevity;

                * * *

Those Chinamen climb toward, and I
Delight to imagine them seated there;
There, on the mountain and the sky,
On all the tragic scene they stare.

                * * *

Their eyes mid many wrinkles, their eyes,
Their ancient, glittering eyes, are gay.

              W. B. Yeats, *Lapis Lazuli*

Lapis Lazuli is the stone of the Medicine Buddha. It is said to have great healing powers. Lapis Lazuli is the great teacher of the mineral kingdom. It teaches us to reach for the sky and dare to dream boldly and with great belief in our own power. Linking our ability to communicate with our intuition, it opens the golden gates to the land of our destiny.

W. B. Yeats had received a piece of lapis lazuli "carved by some Chinese sculptor into the semblance of a mountain with temple, trees, paths, and an ascetic and pupil about to climb the mountain." He wrote of it, "Ascetic, pupil, hard stone, eternal theme of sensual east. The heroic cry in the midst of despair. But no, I am wrong, the east has its solutions always and therefore knows nothing of tragedy. It is we, not the east, that must raise the heroic cry."

11

THE RED RIVER

At twelve, you began to flow
I welcomed you

At thirty-four, you refused to stop
For four years
I cried each time the waters came

Finally, at thirty-eight, you paused
Allowing a new life to grow

For another year
You waited while we nursed
Ignoring my wish that you return

Now, just forty-two,
I must shut you off forever
I am about to bleed for the last time

I will welcome this final ritual bath
The red river shared by all women
I must let you die
So that I may live

SHADES OF BLUE

The Medicine Buddha
Lapis Lazuli – the healing gem
The stone of my ancestral name

Isabel's eyes
Her favorite color
Her stuffed bear

Lake Mah-Kee-Nac
The native turquoise
A healing circle

The complicated sky
Shifting meanings
Shifting moods

The Buddha's healing rays
The sun's healing rays
The radiation aimed at my spine

Feeling blue
Jazz singing to ease the blues

The child-proof medicine bottle
That holds the Tamoxifen

So many shades of blue

DREAM 1: THE GROUP

The small group is disbanding
People are scattering
If I hurry I can join
A few are going toward this support group
The others will form a second

I rush to join the first
Those recently diagnosed
Though my disease has progressed much farther
I feel aligned and similarly situated

I hurry and it is certain
I can make it
I can join

DOES THE BUDDHA PLAY POOL?*

Come Medicine Buddha
Come shine your rays upon me
Penetrate deep within my body
To quell my queasy stomach
And soothe my aching bones

Let those golden arrows
Shoot deep within my frame
Extinguishing the round tumors
That live inside of me

Like a pool cue poised and ready
Aim straight for the triangle
Number 6 in right side pocket
Red 4 to far left corner

Knocking away each colored ball
Dropping steadily into the pockets
Clearing away the hard assortment
Until only white and black remain

The 8 ball holding fast
White blood cell gearing up

And, then, a last shot – and POP!
No more colored balls
The table's cleared

---

*Originally published on line and in print in *Pulse: From the Heart of Medicine*, a collection of poems and essays.

ANGEL'S SONG

I awake to the sound
Of angels singing

The night is quiet
Except for the wind

The angels' voices carry
Over miles, across generations

They sing to heal my pain
They call for me to join them

I feel an aching in my ribs
A sadness in my soul

But the angels' song is beautiful
It is kind and inviting

I know I can give them my hand
Be led on the path of healing

But first, I must acknowledge my pain
Deep and wide

They crossed the River Jordan, and I, too,
Shall arrive safely on the shores of Sangye

FRIDAYS

Friday April 29,
Sue calls me on my cell phone
I am in Bloomingdales
looking at toddlers' spring sundresses

The MRI is not good
You should
see an internist
right away

A weekend of panic:
Will I die before seeing Isabel grow up?
Will I be sick from chemotherapy
her whole childhood?

I think about dying
But also feel content
My only regret
would be leaving Isabel behind

So different from the way I thought I would feel
If told, *You have a year to live*
No conflicts with friends or family to resolve
Satisfaction with my career, no burning desire to travel

Friday May 6,
after a week of bone scans, CT Scans, mammograms,
a double breast MRI,
they find a likely source

Another call on my cell phone
I'm standing over a wine rack

in the crowded
Slope Cellars

The secretary tells me
the bone biopsy will be performed on my pelvis
My pelvis? Did they find a source there?
Yes, several lesions

So it is not only in my spine and ribs
but also in my pelvis
In my state of shock,
I forget that the pelvis is part of this same bony structure

I call Matt,
then Karen
leaving
frantic messages

Matt calls me back
Dr. E says it's nothing new
These are the same lesions we've seen all along
on all the other scans

But
I don't believe him
I call her myself
She reassures me

I picture Georgia O'Keeffe's
paintings of a pelvis
and understand the bone
wraps from front to back

At Audrey's house, while the kids eat ice cream,
she explains female anatomy
I have a pelvis in the other room
She shows me the soft model from her childbirth class

Friday the 13th
The final diagnosis:
Breast Cancer

It has metastasized to my bones

On Saturday,
Isabel and I notice the tulips
outside a bank
in Great Barrington

On Monday, I begin a week of frustrating phone calls
35,000 oncologists are at a conference in Orlando
but by Thursday, I have a first consultation
and on Friday, I meet Dr. V

By the following Monday, he is already busy
setting up appointments for me
first the neurosurgeon to ensure the stability of my spine
then the radiation oncologist to plan my treatment

On Friday May 28,
only a month since it all began,
I sit with Dr. V
in his office

He notices me looking
at the photograph
on his windowsill:
A blond baby girl

Oh, that's not my child, he laughs,
That's the baby of a patient
who was diagnosed
when she was pregnant

I glance back
at the photograph:
The baby is dressed
in a colorful sundress

I think about Isabel waiting for me at home
She will be so excited
to try on the new dress
I bought for her today

THE MONTH OF MAY

May – usually my favorite month
The smell of spring in the air
Warm sun shining brightly
Long days spanning into night

Lilacs in full bloom
Cherry blossoms
Pink and round

My birthday,
Mother's Day,
The start of the summer:
Memorial Day

But this year,
What a different May
News of cancer -
Spreading slowly through my bones

Pain in my back
Tears in my eyes
My usual spring joy
Eclipsed by gripping fear

The saddest *Mother's Day* yet
Of my short-lived
Motherhood

Lying in bed, in pain,
While you played downstairs
With Isabel and Rama

I could not play host
Could barely appreciate the visit
I needed to run and hide
To bury myself deep beneath my blankets

But then you came to me
Ending the fun games
The floor-playing you so adore
To see how you could help

You offered me familiar comfort
Memories of childhood fevers
A damp washcloth cooling my forehead and neck
As you gently stroked my hair

Just as you did years earlier
When I suffered from childhood strep throat
You held back my long hair
As I convulsed over the toilet

No words
Just a loving touch
As only a mother can give

Dream 2: A Gentle Descent

I am flying in an airplane
Emily is asleep in the seat beside me
The plane is moving forward
Steadily and calm

We enter a thick cloud patch
The plane gradually slows
I awaken peacefully to the voice
Of the flight attendant telling us to recline

I understand that we are going down
But there is no panic in the air
I open my eyes to check on Emily
It will be a gentle landing

The plane descends into woods
They are vast and unexplored
But we have room to land
An expansive field spreads wide

The trees remind me
Of that walk through the woods
At Kripalu
So many years ago

NYU and Sloan Kettering

When I describe to friends
The beautiful, new
NYU Clinical Cancer Center
And tell them how I feel supported there,
How going every morning for radiation
Is not even an unpleasant experience,
I always also describe the supportive services provided
The mind/body relaxation workshop
The breast cancer survivors' support group,
Free and open to all patients

This means a lot to me
And I believe it will be instrumental in my healing
I know profoundly that the healing process
Requires far more than medication or radiation
I need to like the facility,
To feel calm when I am there,
To enjoy the shopping in the boutique, where I found the
        perfect camisole,
Which enables me to wear my back brace without a bra

It is so much more welcoming and healing
Than Sloan Kettering was on Tuesday
Disorganized – cold and chaotic – without signs pointing
        the directions
Conflicting instructions about where to find Dr. Schwartz:
On the Lobby Level or Concourse 1
The room where they take insurance information
And have you sign the various consents
Reminded me of an old basement
With paint chipping off the walls

Even the gift shop looked uninviting
Large and commercial – not cozy, warm and welcoming
The labyrinthine waiting rooms
Leaving me confused about where to sit.
Everyone jumbled together
Men and women, young and old
Far-progressed from years of disease
And recently diagnosed

Unlike NYU – small, clean, compact
Clearly marked with signs
Kind attendants, a *concierge* desk
Everything in one building, each on its own floor.
NYU feels caring
It is all about us – the patients
How can they help us recover?
What can they offer to assist our healing?
Sloan Kettering feels like a research center
Everything is a clinical trial
We are the guinea pigs
For their intellectual queries and career advances
I asked for a packet of materials
About what SK provides
No one could direct me to such a thing
A patient said, *you'll find flyers around by the tables*
But even the flyers don't leave me comforted
The two discussing acupuncture don't offer this ancient
practice to help relieve pain
Or assist in the healing process
Instead, they describe research studies:
Does acupuncture speed up recovery?

And, of course, most importantly,
My meeting with Dr. S and the treatment plan
He is smart and moderately warm
In his fifties
Making small talk about the Berkshires
Where he was bike riding last weekend

I thank him for squeezing us into his busy schedule
I tell my story - as I had to Dr. R
(Only Dr.V didn't ask me to repeat this litany
Instead he began our meeting with my medical records
    stacked neatly on his desk
Fully informed about my medical history)

After some discussion, Dr. S brings me in for the exam
Even this is chaotic –
Which exam room should he use?
No specific nurse assigned to assist him
This is not where he usually sees patients.
There is a suitcase in the consultation room
Which leads Matt to ask, *did you just return from a trip?*
Another one of those unreachable oncologists – a researcher
Off giving presentations, not here caring for me
The exam is uneventful
As I know, my neurological functioning is fine

When we finish, we return to the office
Where he pontificates about treatment plans
He says, *Now I will talk for a while*
But interrupt me if I go too fast or speak a foreign language
Nothing he says is new –
The same terms and treatments I have heard repeatedly in
    recent weeks
Not from web research as I had imagined doing
But from Kyle and Fraser

Everything he says is familiar and consistent
Until he gets to the *curve ball*:
A clinical trial in which I might want to participate
The trial involves a novel combination of two treatments
The trial is sponsored by the pharmaceutical company
That developed the drug
The treatment combines an aromatase inhibitor,
About which Kyle had initially told me
But which, in conversations with Dr. R and Dr.V
I learned only works effectively in post-menopausal women

But after my ovarian function is shut down
As a result of the Zoladex monthly injections
Won't I be menopausal and then eligible for the aromatase inhibitor?
No, explains, Dr.V, *because even at that point*
Your ovaries will still produce some estrogen
Undermining the aromatase inhibitors' function

Dr. S answers differently – *after a month, or so*
You will be the same as menopausal
As though your ovaries had been removed
This I believe is wrong –
I also asked about the scenario Dr.V described:
Zoladex shuts down the ovaries temporarily
Puts them in abeyance, on hold
Some research has shown that a premenopausal woman,
      say age 42
Goes on Zoladex for some years
She stays on it past the time she would naturally have entered
      menopause, say 50
And then comes off it at 52
She may begin to ovulate again - her ovaries resuming their
      42-year-old productivity
As they had before the injections

A question for Dr.V
Because the hope, of course, which I now harbor
Is that this scenario could be me
I could shut down my ovaries at 42,
In three years a new and better treatment could be found
A *cure* even,
And this cure might make it safe for me to become
      pregnant again
Then I could stop the Zoladex injections, and resume my cycles
And give birth to miracle baby number 2

I don't think this is feasible or likely
And I am at peace
With Isabel as my only daughter
But someone mentioned Ivy – *who?*

The woman I met at Khari's birthday party whose daughter's
      name is Isabel?
And then I met her again yesterday at Emi's party
Another "*I* " name for a child
And I see that child – *my child*!

Ivy is a stealth grower
Much like my lobular cancer
In fact, it has been analogized to cancer
Growing steadily
Spreading its vine up brick walls
I've always loved Ivy
The lush, green-covered Cornell Quad
The grand buildings of Harvard Yard
Hard stone and brick, softened by nature
I love the fact that ivy covers our house in Brooklyn
It is something I noticed during our first visit
The visit that convinced me this was the home for us
Sunny, bright and light

The conversation with Dr. S continues
He spits out names and writes them on his whiteboard
Chemical names and trade names,
Always careful to note the "*TM* "
My knowledge has advanced so much
Since the meeting with Dr. V
When I had repeatedly interrupted to ask the chemical names
As Kyle had requested that I do
Dr. S draws pictures on the board
Illustrating where the breast ducts are and how ductal and
      lobular cancer spread
But he makes a point of telling me,
At this stage of your disease
The distinction matters little
I learn from Fraser later
And confirm with Dr. V
That this is not quite accurate
The fact that lobular cancer grows sideways in sheets

But more importantly that it is not so blood dependent
Not so fast-growing or dividing.
Particularly in my case
With greater than 90% receptivity to Estrogen and Progesterone
The addiction we need to block
Is to the hormones not the blood

But the new information is certainly something I must consider
Of course I want the best and most effective treatment
However, the newest brilliant hypothesis may not turn out to
       be the best treatment
And because it is experimental, it also poses unknown risks
Why should I be a guinea pig?
My situation is relatively straightforward
My cancer cells appear strongly receptive to Estrogen and Progesterone
So let's start with a first line therapy to block the receptors from their food
I believe this treatment will be highly effective
Dr.V is confident that I will respond well
So long as a well-tested treatment exists
Why experiment with some unknown?

But am I missing an opportunity?
If I don't join the trial now
Will there be an opportunity later for me to benefit from its results?
Will I be in a different place in the future?
Less receptive or responsive to the treatment benefits?
According to Kyle, the greatest difference would be
The years of potential progress I could have made
Were I to start the experimental treatment now,
Particularly if it succeeded in stopping the spread of the cancer

Everyone says the first treatment is the most important
In determining future prognosis
But Tamoxifen should stop the proliferation
It has been tried and worked well in thousands of women
       in my situation
As Fraser explains, *it is the most appropriate first line of defense for*
       a patient like you
What is the rationale for trying this new combination therapy?

Kyle understands the experiment
He is familiar with the receptors
The enzymes and proteins and their reactions
Kyle also knows my unique medical history
My over-reactive autoimmune system
This therapy has many potential harmful side effects
Several that might specifically exacerbate my autoimmune
        conditions
It bothers and worries me
That Sloan Kettering would invite me to join the study
Without taking these factors into consideration
I certainly mentioned them in the consult with Dr. S
And that information was viewed as irrelevant

Moreover, on a personal level,
Although he explained things in clear terms
And spent a long time with Matt and me
It became clear that he was starting to reach the limits of his
        patience
As I took copious notes on the new information, the *curve ball*,
He told me that everything he was saying was also described
In the clinical trial consent form he had given me

I had mentioned that I work at the ACLU
He commented that I was taking a lot of notes
Like a lawyer, he said, with the slightest hint of disdain in his voice

The complete opposite from Dr.V
Who genuinely appreciated my intelligence
My note-taking and question-asking
Telling me all the chemical names of compounds,
As Kyle had requested
And going beyond this
Offering on his own, *Kyle is free to call me*
If you would like to have him call
Which Kyle did, and had a long and thorough conversation,
With Dr.V explaining details of the aromatase inhibitors
About which Kyle still had questions

Kyle liked him very much
Thought he was nice, smart and warm
And Dr.V said nice things about me
Telling Kyle and Fraser he liked me
Thought I was very smart
During our consultation I noted his pleasant surprise
At my knowledge (learned from Kyle) of bisphosphonates

Dr.V is always available
Returning a call to my cell phone himself
Feel free to stop by after radiation
Checking in after weekend calls to his on-call colleagues
One day I see him in the waiting room
When I am on the fourth floor to schedule an appointment
He puts his hand gently on mine and asks,
How's everything going?
And he remembers, as he must with hundreds of patients,
My precise protocol:
You'll begin the Tamoxifen on Thursday, right?

Claire, Dr. E and others told me
That my oncologist would become my best friend
Like a husband, Claire said
I appreciate and understand this
And believe I have found my healing partner
I trust him inherently
I know that I am in good hands
There is a softness to his Midwestern roots
A gentleness that comes through
He was raised in Iowa

Matt and I loved the story he told about *Nigel*
And the advice he had given to our friends Frazer and Luisa
Who had wanted to name their son, *Nigel*
But Dr.V told them this would be an awful name
For a kid growing up in Texas
He gave this advice as perhaps only a non-New Yorker could
Someone familiar with small towns,

31

With landlocked regions of our country
Someone who likely stood out among his friends
Smart, driven, yet still gentle

So I am content
I know that I have found the best doctor
The best facility
I am grateful to Claire for speaking so highly of NYU
And also glad her brilliant doctor, Dr. P
Who saved her life,
Was not available or not willing to see me
Not able to take on a new patient
He was on call this past weekend
So I met him by telephone:
Clearly smart and a respected authority
But also curt and a bit dismissive

I know that I need someone who is caring
With whom I can be myself
Express my fears
And he will comfort me
Not talk down to me
Not dismiss my concerns

I know I have found that in Dr. V
And at NYU
This is the choice I am making
And I know it will serve me well

DREAM 3: SUBWAY

I am in the subway
Traveling downtown
I am on my way to 34th Street
To NYU

I have my big, blue-striped bag
Filled with my notebooks, Buddhist texts, a jacket
A woman gets in and wants to sit next to me
She is older and more frail for her years than she should be
Slightly disheveled, disorganized, hunched over

I move my stuff to make room for her to sit down
My jacket, its shiny rain-slicker fabric, sticks out of my bag
I pull it back in to clear the seat for her
But she pulls it back – she wants it between us
To sit on and keep herself dry

Just as I comprehend that she wants to share my jacket,
Take her own protection from my protective gear,
I realize that the train has stopped at 34th Street
My exit

I grab my belongings and rush
To get out before the doors close
I glance back toward my seat
To make sure I have all my things

I sense that I have left something behind
But I cannot see it
I cannot open my eyes
I panic, calling to the other passengers,
Is something left behind?

A man notices something but won't hand it to me
Still with my eyes closed,
I grasp out frantically
I beg, *Please give me my things before the doors close!*

This is 34th Street,
I need to get out
To go to the NYU Clinical Cancer Center!
I am not well, I need my medication!

They will think I'm crazy
So I say, *I'm a psychologist*
Please pass me my things
Calmly and professionally
But still no one moves

I realize I would accomplish my goal
More easily
Be able to get my bag
And leave the train
If I would just open my eyes

But I can't open my eyes
And I fear that the doors will close
Trapping me inside
Or I will rush from the train
Leaving part of myself behind

NEGLIGEE

Do you remember the negligee you bought for me
Along with the silk underwear
A gift from Victoria's Secret
So many years ago?

Do you remember the New Year's Eve
When we left the bellowing Chuck Berry
To return to your apartment
And dance shirtless to our own music?

And of course the two bottles
Of red zinfandel
The cheese and crackers and blanket
While the New York Philharmonic performed in Central Park

At the café, we played footsie under the table
I like women with long hair, you said
Remembering, perhaps, the hair of my adolescence
But ignoring my present short crop

You took a bus to Cape Cod
To join Amy and me at our summer rental
She with her new boyfriend, Garrett
And I with you

I met you at the station
We drove to a sandy cove
Kissing under the stars
To the sound of the waves

A perfect vacation at the beach
Long walks along the water's edge

Collecting rocks and sea shells
Sharing our most-intimate secrets

For no apparent reason
I told you about my family's long-running debate:
My father wanted to be cremated,
My mother wanted a graveside at which to mourn

I was reading *Beloved*
Another strange premonition of ghosts
But none of it felt threatening
I am the happiest I've ever been

We drove back to Boston on Saturday
Eating clam rolls on the way
To spend a final weekend together
Before law school and your job pulled us apart

But then the world crashed down on me
I was awakened Sunday morning by the phone
My mother's tear-soaked voice, *Daddy had a heart attack*
He died while running a 5K race

In shock, I collapsed in the corner
We had to hurry   pack   find something black to wear
      Call a cab   get to the airport   fly to New York
All in a blur   your parents waiting for us at Laguardia

You stuck by me through that weekend
Shepherding relatives back and forth
Walked with me in the evenings
As I searched for words to express my grief

And you stuck by me after that weekend
Through the difficult months that followed
When depression darkened my days
And sadness consumed my nights

Our love was so young then
Our romance so new, unformed

You had no obligation to stay
Most men would have run and hidden

But not you
You stayed
    Giving   loving   supporting   me
Even when I failed to reciprocate

You knew we had something special
You were determined to let it grow
And it did grow
Through weeks   months   seasons

Now the years add up to seventeen
Almost the age we were when it began
And still you stand by me
And love me body and soul

RICK

Might I see you
On the other side?

The side you so adamantly
Refused to admit existed

But Einstein believed
In the mystery of the universe

Carl Sagan saw
The depth and breadth of the cosmos

You, yourself, were fascinated by the fourth dimension
Where time and space merge

I miss you so much at times
The tears well up out of nowhere

From a reference in a book
Or a character in a play

You are here, so present
Though so much has changed since you've been gone

Kyle has two children
You are my daughter's namesake

I am a lawyer at the ACLU
Fighting for social justice

The commitment you instilled in me
From an early age

I'm still so proud of you
And brag about you often

My father was a scientist
A McCarthy delegate, an artist

He drove a motorcycle
Loved to scuba dive

How I wish you could see me now
How proud you would be of the person I've become

And how I wish you could be with me now
Help me with all that I am going through

So different from your sudden death
Maybe not death at all

CLEAN SHEETS

Against one's skin
Pulled taught
Around the edges
Soft yet firm

No wrinkles
No bunches
An ocean of smooth silk

Like the ones in the best hotels
    In Paris
        London
  Or Rome

Is that it?
The fancy hotels of memory?
Or is it more fundamental?

The smoothness of skin
The coolness of a mother's hand
On a feverish forehead

To be held
To be comforted
Contained

Between cool cotton
      Freshly washed
  Tightly tucked
Sheets

I NEED TO BE HELD

I   need   to   be   held

To feel your arms
Strong and comforting
Quieting my busy mind

It   is   not   enough
To hold Isabel

To calm and quiet her

As she tosses and turns tonight

I   need   you   to   quiet   me

It   is   not   enough

To lie here focusing on my breathing

It   is   not   enough
I need your touch

Skin warming skin
I know you need your sleep
You have been

Giving so much

Still

I   need   this   one   thing   more
I need not to be alone
In the middle of the night

When I should be sleeping, dreaming
Will you sometimes be awake too?
Then fall back to sleep easily,
With me in your arms?

BIRDS

In a dream I see a woman on a park bench
The birds flock all around her
Gentle birds   singing birds
Parakeets and yellow finches

Matt's and Betsy's pet birds
Colorful parrots roaming freely through their apartments
The birds who visit the feeder
Outside our window in the Berkshires

The birds in my dream sing
Their melodies are distinct but merge with one another
Slightly different songs   the calls of different species
Create a chorus of sound

Matt recognizes bird calls
He asks me, *Do you hear the Cardinal?*
I never even noticed that birds have different languages
Until that morning on Cape Cod

I'm learning their voices now

From our garden in Brooklyn
Our yard in the Berkshires

From the little stuffed Audubon birds
Isabel received as baby presents

And now, the first Mourning Dove
Coos outside my window
The sky is still dark, but this one wakes early

When I began writing

I noticed the silence
I listened for a melody, but heard none

Then for a moment I heard the call of a Cardinal
Outside my window
In the trees in our backyard
And in the garden next door

The birds flock there   unexpectedly
A sanctuary in the middle of Brooklyn
Is it our cherry tree that beckons them?
Or the magnolia tree next door?

Now it is quiet again
Just one lone bird calling out to me
Telling me the angels are silent tonight
But the birds, at least, are with me

As night wanes into morning
A second bird appears
I hear the call and the response
To each other, not to me

But I am here with them
Awake at my favorite hour
When the birdcalls dominate the city sounds
Until the Tai Chi music floats in from next door

The birds are awake

Now a car drives by
Soon the sky will lighten and turn pink
As it did that morning before Isabel was born

Signaling a new day, a new life

I suppose I should accept it and stay awake
Rachel said, *It's fine to be up in the middle of the night*
so long as you take a nap later

Let me try once more
At least until 5:00 a.m.

I'll let the bird songs be my lullaby
They can sing me back to sleep

But now the chorus is too loud
Like a symphony orchestra tuning up
It is difficult to distinguish the individual birdcalls
Among the cacophony of song

So I am awake

But I am grateful for their song
The song that sings to me
The song that is my guide

AURORA

I didn't realize my connection
To the flowers all around
But now I see them everywhere
In my art work   my internet password

The flower essences that heal
Not even picked, so as not to hurt them
Just bent over the water
To share their energy

I've thought about hurting flowers
Wondered whether I should press them anymore
But flowers regenerate   re-grow
In fact, need trimming to flourish

If I don't pull out the root
The bloom can reappear
Perhaps fuller
And richer than before

Aurora – the healing flower held
In the Medicine Buddha's right hand
Aurora Healing Arts
The name of my next daughter:

Aurora Ivy
And there will be one
I will not only be the first Stage 4 cured
My preserved ovaries will again bear fruit

Isabel and I will pick flowers together
She learned how to plant them

With Matt in our backyard in Brooklyn
With Grandma and Poppy in the Berkshires

Even *Poppy* is a flower
A name Isabel devised on her own
We always called him *Grandpa*
But she chose the name to call him

I will teach her to hold them gently
So as not to damage them
And to use the glue sparingly
We'll make a beautiful collage

THE MUSE

The muse departs
but she does not wander far away
only far enough
to give me time to sleep
replenish my resources
so I can be strong again

A night bursting with eight poems
followed by a day of exhaustion
and a determination, an intention
to sleep

The newer ones have been richer
deeper and more concrete
universal in their meaning
less explicit in their text

With the help of a pill
I now sleep for many hours,
two nights in a row
and awaken feeling refreshed

But I am confident she will return
I will have more to say
I have more to say already,
as you can see

SHIN/DAWN

As you finished my facial
You asked if people were drawn to me
If people like me
I said, *I suppose so*
You asked, *Do you know why?*
I responded, *Why?*
You said, *No you tell me*
I said, *Perhaps because I am becoming a healer*

You said,
You are healing yourself from within
You seem so healthy,
You have a glow around you
A positive energy that draws people in

I said, *Maybe it is the Reiki energy*
That people are sending my way
I asked if you were Japanese
You said, *No Korean*
I told you of my interest in the Medicine Buddha
Tibetan Buddhism
And my desire to go to Japan
To visit a Zen Buddhist monastery

I talked about Chinese medicine
And Eastern philosophy
Being so far ahead of the West
How American doctors just want
To prescribe drugs or cut off body parts

I spoke of Chinese medicine principles
Working to heal from within

Working with the body to heal itself
In its infinite wisdom to do so

I asked what Shin translates to
You responded,
Dawn

Dawn, I said
That is beautiful
I love the dawn,
It is my favorite time of day

It is the time I compose my poems
It is the time I did Tai Chi

Only later, in a conversation with the owner
Did I learn that you practice Reiki.
The owner has been receiving Reiki energy from you
Three times a week
To heal injuries from an accident

A terrible, freak accident:
She had been walking in Prospect Park
And emerged from the woods
Just as two horses were rounding a corner
She got trampled, and broke hundreds of bones

She is healing now
And you've been helping her through Reiki
But you were much too humble
To mention that to me

What started as a facial
Turned into so much more
I will have to return soon

ISABEL'S BIRTH

I awoke at 5:00 a.m.
looked out my window and saw

      the   most   beautiful   pink   sunrise

I had ever seen

I thought to myself,

> *My baby girl is on the way*
> *She will be here soon*

I was so excited,
the process had begun

But a visit to my doctor
quashed my enthusiasm

This is nothing
Don't expect the baby for a week
Stop counting contractions
Go get a stress test

I was so upset
I had been sure the baby was coming
And now, I was told that what I felt was

      false   *labor*

Braxton Hicks contractions
I should ignore them

But a call to my doula, Chris,
reassured me that what I felt was real

that things had started happening
and this was all part of the process

I went to work and stayed until 8:00 p.m.
My contractions intensified throughout the day
That night I could not get comfortable
and I cried thinking,

>*If I can't even take this pain*
>*How will I ever handle actual labor?*

I was so disappointed
The natural childbirth I had yearned for
now seemed impossible

All through the night I sat in the rocking chair,
My contractions strengthened and became more rapid

But I failed to realize
because the doctor had misled me

I   WAS   IN   LABOR

By the morning, the pain was so intense
I called Chris and the doctor

Chris said she would come over right away
She suggested that I take a Benadryl
and a warm bath
She said I should relax and get some sleep

I called the doctor
Dr. E's partner took the call
He asked about the contractions and the timing in between
I explained they had been closer
but now had slowed

He said, *You can come in if you want to*
but I don't recommend it

>*It   doesn't   sound   like   you   are   close*

He sanctioned my taking Benadryl
He said it would not harm the baby

Chris came over
And helped me into the bath
She gave me the Benadryl
and sat on the edge of my bed
as I dozed in and out of sleep

Matt had to go to a meeting
He promised he'd be back by noon
Neither of us thought this would be the day
that our baby would be born

But as the day progressed,
the contractions intensified
and the gaps between shortened

I sat in bed, resting
Chris sat at my feet
comforting me,
bringing me food
and reading to herself while I rested

She had to go see another client –
        I later learned the client was Robin,
        a friend I would meet the following September at
        mommy baby yoga,
                who   by coincidence
shared my doula and obstetrician

After I had rested for some time,

        eating   sleeping

Matt returned to sit by my side

We watched silly romantic comedies
and chatted idly to pass the time

As the movies played on
the contractions came more frequently

<pre>
    Deep   Strong   Fast
</pre>

The intervals between   shorter

Like the tide,
rolling in and out,
a contraction would wash over me

<pre>
     One   Two   Three   Four   Five
</pre>

Keeping time with the rolling credits

Then I lost the plug
And I knew it was almost time
I told Matt, *We are going to the hospital tonight*
He asked, *Are you sure?*
I said, *I know it will be tonight*
<pre>
          Let's   get   ready
</pre>

I called Chris to come over
She helped me into the bath
I could barely walk

The pauses between   so   short
The contractions

OVERWHELMING!

We called the doctor
She remained skeptical

Put Lenora on the phone

Chris handed me the phone
After a few seconds of conversation
another contraction washed over me
and I dropped the phone into Chris' hands

Let me hear her sounds

Chris held the phone close to my mouth
and I bellowed

Deep   Loud   Strong

Full of birthing sound

Dr. E recognized the sound and shouted,

I want you to come to the hospital –

IMMEDIATELY!

She knew I was close
despite her having told me yesterday
that I had not dilated at all,
that I was barely effaced
that the baby wouldn't come for another week

I showered quickly
called to Matt to pack the bag

    Get the baby seat from the basement!

    We   were   so   unprepared

It was six days before my due date

Although I had wanted to organize everything
the weekend before
Matt had resisted setting up the car seat
saying, *We'll do it next weekend*

    Now   there   was   no   time

We gathered things together quickly
throwing everything into the hospital bag
including, by mistake, our portable phone

We ran out of the house

We later learned from our neighbors
that we had left our door wide open
on a Friday night in Brooklyn

Matt brought the car around from somewhere

while Chris helped me down the steps
I wanted the pillow from my bed
Matt ran back up to get it

Throughout the car ride my contractions intensified

       Deep   Guttural   Strong

I remembered the woman I had seen
giving birth in the fields in Kenya

Chris told me to keep the moans low
So as not to push

       Will you moan with me, I asked

Chris sat in the back seat with me
I kneeled facing backwards
clenching the headrest
and the pillow from my bed

Matt drove fast but in control
appearing calm despite his panic

Luckily, the Friday night traffic was light
as we flew up the FDR Drive

We made it to the hospital

         in   half   an   hour

Matt said he would park the car

As I got out a contraction hit

        I   doubled   over

Chris and I started to walk inside
I could barely walk
An attendant offered me a wheel chair
       No she'll walk, Chris answered

We got inside and another contraction hit

Deep   Hard

I grabbed a wall to steady myself
I knew it would be soon

We made it to the elevator
and up to the 11th floor
As the doors opened

      I   was   overcome   again

I held tightly to the door of the elevator
as a contraction almost floored me

Dr. E was there   waiting
When the contraction subsided
she grabbed my hand
and dragged me to the delivery room

We rushed
past the nurses
who wanted insurance information

My husband will be here soon,
He'll give you what you need,
I called over my shoulder

We rushed into the delivery room
The nurses wanted to hook me up
Dr. E yelled, *She doesn't need anything*
She is fine on her own!

Let's check you quickly, Dr. E said
I was 9 centimeters dilated

      Ready   To   Give   Birth

But my water hadn't broken
(The only reason I didn't have the baby in the car)

With my permission,
Dr. E broke my water

57

She told me I could push

I didn't want to lie on the bed
flat on my back
so we tried other positions

I remembered Ellen mentioning the toilet
I sat on the cold porcelain
I started to push

    The   *baby's*   *head*   *crowned*

Dr. E said, *I can't catch the baby*
with you sitting on the toilet

I tried lying on the bathroom floor
but it was
                  cold   hard   uncomfortable

Chris suggested going on all fours

      on my hands and knees

      on the bed

I liked this position and felt strongly secure

    I   *PUSHED!*

After just three pushes, Isabel came out

    My beautiful baby girl!

We had arrived at the hospital at 9:30 pm
At 10:20

    She   Was   Born

Dr. E asked Matt if he wanted to cut
the umbilical cord
He said, *no*

She asked if I would like to cut it
I said *yes,*   immediately

We lay Isabel on the bed
between my spread legs
as I hovered over her
still on my hands and knees

I   cut   the   cord

They helped me lie down on the bed
and handed her to me
Chris helped me start to nurse
and Isabel latched on immediately

Her little mouth

    sucked   sucked

As she still does in her sleep
tiny puckering movements
her little lips grabbing for nourishment
                comfort

I lay there with my newborn

    Happy   Content

A beautiful birth, a beautiful baby
A new life   had begun

A Cup of Tea

A cup of tea
from the Cameron Highlands
Boh – Thailand
given to me by Lama

Its heat and steam
forces me to slow down

    breathe   in

Hold the moment

Like Lama himself

    quiet   yet   profound

Compelling me to   slow   down

    listen

    breathe

    heal

Through words and compassion

You will live a long life
You will be all right

I drink my tea
tasting its freshness

Picked each morning
from the Highlands

I travel there in my mind
to join others

I appreciate the

tea

the moment

the   simple   things

I realize
how profound
simplicity can be

THE TREES, THE HILLS

The trees, the hills:
Take a good look
Breathe them in
The morning elements:
Experience them
Taste them
Hold them

Grounded   Old

So tall,
having grown for decades
So sure of themselves
unmarred by life's challenges

Their purpose
          to   grow
To reach for the sky
The heavens
No other purpose
than to be here

          Fully   Present

And yet, what power they bring
What wisdom they can teach us

We, too, can grow

          Tall   Sturdy

Strong   within ourselves
Grounded   in the Earth

REIKI

Deep   relaxation

Floating
    in   out

A vision of giraffes

    a mother and her colt
on the African plains

Later,
      the ocean
    wide stretches of open beach

  the   waves
      breaking   breaking

Rolling   rolling,
   for miles

Thoughts
    of   Isabel
      of   Matt

of the everyday world

Then no thoughts at all

     just   floating

Somewhere deep,
   somewhere calm

Now feeling
     your   hands   upon   me

gentle   warm

A light touch
     behind   my   head

Under my back
     on   my   stomach

Now   your hands   disappear

I am confused,
  Are you still touching me?

Or have
     your   hands
          moved   elsewhere?

Your voice:
     at first
          calm   soothing

Urging me to go deep
to find that place

  that   place   beyond   words

Beyond   worldly   senses

So, I went
I went

     deep

I went

     far

I traveled the world

  this   world   and   other   worlds

I saw:
  people
    animals

I   felt   sounds
   heard   colors
     touched   feelings

You circled the rim of the bowl
     the vibrations rang

First one note
        then   another

A signal to return
to come back
       to   this   world
 this reality

But
    slowly   slowly

      gently

  letting go

     while still holding on

Bringing the serenity with me

    into   the   everyday   world

And you told me,
   It is always there
   with you

    IT   *IS*   *YOU*

I can reach for it
I can attain it
I can carry it with me

   A L W A Y S

Through the Twilight

Since we were little girls
you felt the pull
the Ouigi board and Tarot cards

I followed you
played along
but always held back

You studied Eastern religions
joined an Ashram in the west
became part of a Sangha

You recognized and acknowledged
your own pain
and determined to help ease the pain of others

You studied medicine
but knew you needed to connect
the healing with the heart

You moved toward alternatives
studied flower essences
and Mayan uterine massage

Helping women,
healing women
you followed your calling

You found others
who spoke the language
of the spirit world

When I was in pain

aching for a child
you led me to Rachel

When I was pregnant
you comforted me with herbs
made me tinctures

When I told you of
the excruciating pain in my back
you led me to Susan

You reassured me about chiropractors
told me about your own back pain
supported me as I sobbed

When I learned I might have cancer
you were the friend I called
you took Isabel without question

When the news was not good
you said,
Life is not fair

You spoke to me
from a place of honesty
naming truth at its core

On one dark morning, when I was exhausted
from hours on the phone, you came over
You gave me the card of Mary Beth Augustine

But you sensed I needed more
You understood that I could not be alone
I was unraveling

So you kept me close by your side
You took me home and fed me lunch
You accompanied me at my appointments

I want to share more:
the medical and physical, the emotional
and creative, the spiritual and holistic

I know you are there,
deeply in tune,
with all that I am feeling

As you will be
always, and
I am forever grateful

THE PLAYGROUP

We began when you were just six weeks old
A tiny newborn entering the world
At the birth of the New Year –
Rosh Hashana

Because it was a holiday
Nick joined Laura and Josh
I noticed them immediately
Her sunburst tattoo etched large and deep

At first you lay on the mat beside me
Barely moving at all
Just crying out when thirst or hunger
Demanded my attention

Soon you were lifting your head
A milestone!   A maturation!
Next, you rolled over
From front to back, then back to front

Scarlett led the way
Exploring everyone's mats
The curious, adorable baby
We all hoped ours would become

Soon you who could sit started gathering
In the center of the room
On yoga blankets with toys
Scott kept you entertained

Then the sitters started crawling
You were among the first

Going from water bottle to bright toy
Amusing all the yogis

Soon the crawlers became walkers
At nine months I proudly announced
You had taken your first step
Uttered your first word:

Bird

What more beautiful first word could be uttered?
We went around the room
Introducing ourselves through song

    Wind up, wind up,
    wind up, Isabel

My favorite part
Was deep relaxation

    An oxymoron in a room filled with babies

I lay on my side on the mat
With a blanket at my side
I held you close to my heart
So we could nurse and descend together

The lunch ritual began soon after
My second or third class
I asked if I might
Join the other moms

We brought sandwiches to the Conservatory garden
Laura, Robin, Kris and I
A filmmaker, a teacher, an artist, a lawyer
We were all moms who were more than moms

Later we had lunches at the Olive Vine
We grew closer as our children grew older
We connected at a level

That felt
  new   *deep*   *rich*

Through the summer at the
  Tot Lot

You grew:
  from a baby
      into toddler

Your friends:
  Josh   Caleb   Stella

Your friendships grew
Stronger as we moved from
        yoga   *to*   *playgroup*
And now, nearly three years later
We still meet in the park on Fridays
We put our blankets together
And share our children and our lives

ACCEPTANCE

I didn't know you worried
I suppose I should have assumed you cried
But you never show it
Never break

I learn through others
The questions you've been storing
Hiding away
Guarding from me

What are you trying to protect?
Why do you believe silence is better?
Who taught you that being strong
Means never showing your weaknesses?

Was it your father's death when you were only six?
That pivotal moment in your life
A child's confused emotions
    You're too young to attend the funeral

So you learned to be strong
To pretend to be a grown up.
    Grown ups don't cry
Grown ups don't get scared

But we need to cry
To purge   release
Catharsis is a natural healing
Until it comes   we are blocked

Vulnerability is true strength
Accepting fear and sadness helps to overcome

By looking fear in the eye   welcoming it
We learn that we are stronger than it seems

Like a bear in the woods
Or a snake in the grass
If we run away they will run toward us
They fear us just as we fear them

But if we keep still
Open up and feel our fear
Stare them in the eye
With a strength that says

     I   *will*   *not*   *run*

Then they too will sit quietly
Their fear will subside alongside ours
We each will learn the other is not a threat
Just another being in this vast universe

THE PATH TOWARD HEALING

I first came to you
to help heal

    the   void   of   infertility

You believed in me
saw an inner strength
that I was yet to realize

For years
you sat by my side
confident that

    a   baby   would   come

You nourished my spirit
my pottery, tai chi,

    my love of Kripalu   the Berkshires

You spoke of
Buddhist beliefs
gave me a copy of

    When Things Fall Apart

But I was not ready
to comprehend
the deep healing
that suffering can bring

I come to you now
with an even deeper pain
in need of greater healing

But also with an understanding
of the healing power
that pain can bring

You shared with me

> *The   Medicine   Buddha*

You offered to teach me the practice

> I   think   I   am   ready

Now I see the signs:

> *Lapis Lazuli,*
>
> > *The   Medicine   Buddha*

My last name:
> *Lapidus*

My first name:
> *Lenora*

Like the Buddha's healing rays
The sun's aura

Could I be destined for

> the   path   of   a   *Bodhisattva?*

In a moment of self-pity

> I   cried:

> > *My father's early death*
> > *My years of infertility*
> > *My newly discovered cancer*

Then I realized that the hardship
was a signpost:

I should do
> something   important   with   my   life

You said,
   You ARE doing something important with your life

Again you acknowledged and affirmed

        the   good   within   me

which you so often recognize
long before I do

I told you of the
        loving   kindness

I had received from
friends and family

The gift box filled with lotions
        the generosity that surprised me

You said,
   It   is   no   coincidence,
        you   have   created   that

You always approach me
with that perfect balance
of Western reason
and Eastern spirit

Never pushing too hard
Accepting my skepticism
but seeing my slow movement
toward the light

        And   now   I   am   ready

You offered to guide me

The Commentaries state that guidance
is a necessary precondition
to penetrate the twilight
to open up to clarity

The Commentaries state,

a   *Bodhisattva*
     endures   *unheard*   *of*   *hardships*

I am grateful for the
    patience   *compassion*

you have shown me
these past seven years

And the offer to lead me
along the path of healing

     deeper   *in*

ABOUT THE AUTHOR

Lenora Lapidus is the Director of the Women's Rights Project at the American Civil Liberties Union. She litigates gender discrimination cases in federal and state courts throughout the country, engages in public policy advocacy, participates in international human rights mechanisms, and speaks on gender equity issues in the media and to the public. Her work focuses on economic justice, educational equity, ending violence against women, and addressing women's human rights to health, housing and safety. In June 2013, she won a unanimous ruling from the U.S. Supreme Court in *AMP v. Myriad Genetics* striking down Myriad's patents on the human BRCA genes, which are associated with breast and ovarian cancer. Lenora received a JD from Harvard Law School and a BA from Cornell University.

Lenora lives in Park Slope, Brooklyn, with her husband Matt Bialer (a literary agent, poet, photographer, and painter) and their 11-year-old daughter Izzy.